a breed apart

a

breed apart

a celebration of **the new american mutt**

photographs by amanda jones

clarkson potter/publishers
new york

Library of Congress
Cataloging-in-Publication Data
Jones, Amanda.
A breed apart : a celebration of the
new American mutt / photographs by
Amanda Jones.
1. Mutts (Dogs)—United States—Pictorial
works. 2. Photography of dogs. I. Title.
SF430.J66 2007
636.7—dc22   2006051562

ISBN 978-0-307-34675-9

Printed in the United States of America

Design by Jane Treuhaft

10 9 8 7 6 5 4 3 2 1

First Edition

for savannah, a breed apart who is worlds apart

acknowledgments

For Elissa Altman, who had the confidence to help get this book off the ground, we are extremely grateful. Thank you for believing in our work.

To all of the owners of the *A Breed Apart* models, thank you for your time and effort.

To Christine Enderle, whose enthusiasm, organization, and professionalism made the production of *A Breed Apart* go smoothly, thank you.

nellie

callie

lenny

fore**word**

Mixed-breed. Mongrel. Heinz 57. All-American. Mutt. Would a dog by any other name smile as sweet? You may be surprised to learn that the most popular—or, shall I say, most prevalent—type of dog in America currently is a mixed-breed. There are more mutts in American homes than any single breed—more than Labs, Golden Retrievers, and Yorkies (who rank two, three, and four, respectively). That's saying something.

As a lifelong devotee of mutts, I completely understand America's current fascination. What better candidate could there be for first-place honors in a country that proudly claims to be the world's melting pot? For almost ten years now, my job has allowed me to meet wonderful dogs, many of them of "uncertain parentage." Where do I start to sing their praises?

One of the great pleasures of life with a mutt is the game we all play: trying to determine our dog's particular heritage, and thus her traits and personality. A Retriever? A Spaniel? Is that a Hound's howl? The wonderful thing about mixes is that they possess a delightful mélange of traits—the sociability of a Beagle, perhaps, and the attention to detail of a Border Collie—like my Nell, a little mixed-breed (Border Beagle!) who came to us as a foundling, and who changed my life and inspired me to start *The Bark* magazine. People stop me all the time, asking, "What kind of dog is she?" I've been assured that she's part Pit Bull, Border Collie, Hound, and Spaniel (look at her webbed feet!). I'm pleased that she can claim such diverse ancestry. It makes her all that more special—a true one-of-a-kind dog! A couturiere original, sui generis of her species!

My life with dogs goes way back. Nathan and Chaka were my co-pilots during my organic-apple-farming days in the 1970s; Nathan was a high-jumping Standard Poodle/German Shepherd, and Chaka was a Lab/Irish Setter. After a hiatus, dogs reentered my life when we got Nellie, who inspired us to organize a dog park in Berkeley, California, coin our motto, "Dog Is My Co-Pilot," and launch the magazine. Callie, a wise and soulful Husky mix, joined our pack in increments, gravitating toward our home from down the block until we officially adopted her. She was smart as a whip and gentle as a lamb. Lenny, a Terrier mix, came home with me one day after I visited our local animal control shelter; his spirit cried out for companionship and I couldn't refuse. Each dog has all the traits of their respective stock: Nell, a herder and a clown, nose always close to the ground and prone to an ancestral howl now and then; Callie, calm and intelligent, the true magnanimous alpha who never needs to assert her status, positively radiating noblesse oblige; and Lenny, attentive, exuberant, and energetic, with a true Terrier nature—always ready.

If every dog has its day, let's hope that it's the mutt's turn now. Even though all dogs originally came from mixed-breed stock eons ago, mutts have played second fiddle to their more high-bred brethren for too long now! The idiosyncratic charms of the dogs in this book speak volumes for the love they share with their humans. Plus, who doesn't root for an underdog?

—**Claudia Kawczynska**, cofounder and editor of *The Bark* magazine

schn**oodle**

(schnauzer + poodle)

tyler, greenbrae, ca

lelaina, tulsa, ok

bullbrador

(pit bull + labrador)

borgi

(border collie + welsh corgi)

deagle

(dachshund + beagle)

walter, san francisco, ca

bindi, portland, me

colita

(border collie + akita)

daphne, williamstown, ma

spanden

(goۅden retriever + spaniel)

molly, new york, ny

puggle

(pug + beagle)

spanieletter

(spaniel + setter)

savannah, adams, ma

lucy, williamstown, ma

sheprador

(german shepherd + labrador)

goldendoodle

(golden retriever + poodle)

scott**anese**

(scottish terrier + havanese)

henry, asheville, nc

spike, brooklyn, ny

russenji

(jack russell + basenji)

nea**nard**

(saint bernard + neapolitan mastiff)

ralphie, boulder, co

english **letter**

(labrador + english setter)

cocka**poo**

(cocker spaniel + poodle)

shepland

(german shepherd + newfoundland)

labraden

(black labrador + golden retriever)

pit**bullet**

(pit bull + basset hound)

vasco, new york, ny

nita franchesca, houston, tx

piggy

(pug + italian greyhound)

moyeden

(golden retriever + samoyed)

rahuahua

(rat terrier + chihuahua)

myles, oak park, il

schnauzer**min**

(schnauzer + mini doberman)

newby, tulsa, ok

eskipoo

(eskimo + poodle)

dachenshunder

(dachshund + golden retriever)

patterford

(patterdale terrier + staffordshire terrier)

clarence, new york, ny

rhoundback

(rhodesian ridgeback + greyhound)

anya, williamstown, ma

sp**ollie**

(border collie + spaniel)

billy, new york, ny

jackodauzer

(jack russell + poodle + schnauzer)

philamina, fayetteville, ny

silkihund

(silky terrier + dachshund)

doxador

(labrador + dachshund)

chobe**rotti**

(doberman + chow + rottweiler)

biscuit and toasty, miami, fl

golden rollie

(golden retriever + border collie)

labrahound

(black labrador + greyhound)

deaglehund

(basset hound + beagle + dachshund)

chackh**ussell**

(chihuahua + jack russell)

gidget, brooklyn, ny

m**ug**gin

(mini pinscher + pug)

dakota, north adams, ma

igge**raner**

(weimaraner + italian greyhound)

better **collie**

(border collie + english setter)

murphy, williamstown, ma

borkie

(bichon + yorkshire terrier)

sk**errier**

(skye terrier + norfolk terrier)

sheagle

(beagle + german shepherd)

spanollie

(french spaniel + border collie)

chloé, woodstock, ny

schippier

(schipperke + terrier)

gracie, brecksville, oh

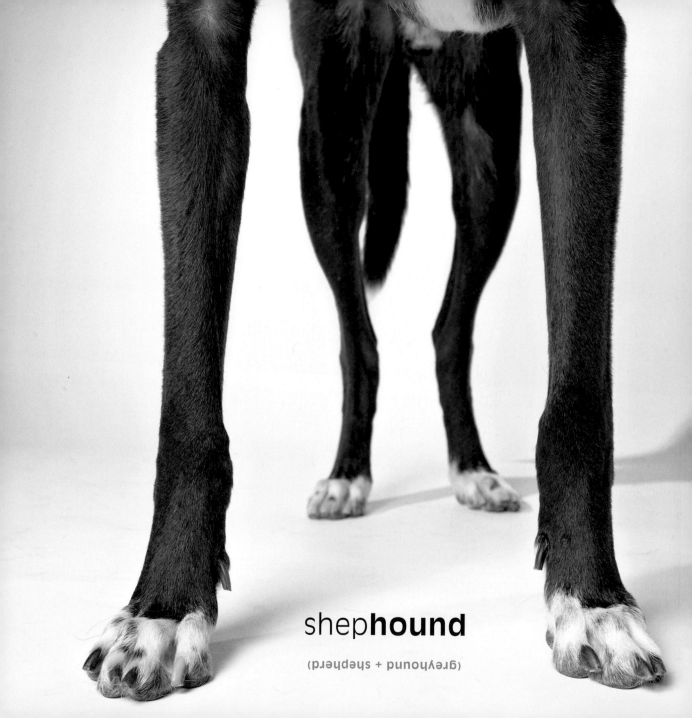

shep**hound**

(greyhound + shepherd)

turkish, gates mills, oh

zoe, berkeley, ca

labradoodle

(labrador + poodle)

gollie

(border collie + golden retriever)

rudy, new york, ny

blubrador

(labrador + blue healer)

sadie, glenview, il

huskador

(labrador + husky)

bord**eltie**

(sheltie + border collie)

golden**nese**

(golden retriever + great pyrennese)

tommy, san francisco, ca

albert, vorhees, nj

bullshire terrier

(american staffordshire terrier + bulldog)

ausollie

(border collie + australian shepherd)

millie maxine, chittenango, ny

pooky

(yorkshire terrier + poodle)

labra**dane**

(great dane + labrador)

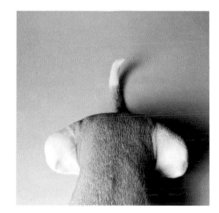

bulmation

(pit bull + dalmation)

?

(¿ + ¿ + ¿ + ¿)

P9-DEZ-476

DATE	ISSUED TO
05	GRO
05	NEW
APR 1 3 2006	mcgr
07	NEVA

© DEMCO 32-2125

Digby and Kate 1, 2, 3

Digby

1

DUTTON CHILDREN'S BOOKS ○ NEW YORK

and Kate

BY Barbara Baker

PICTURES BY Marsha Winborn

For Judy Herman
B.A.B.

Text copyright © 2004 by Barbara A. Baker
Illustrations copyright © 2004 by Marsha Winborn
All rights reserved.
CIP Data is available.
Published in the United States 2004 by Dutton Children's Books,
a division of Penguin Young Readers Group
345 Hudson Street, New York, New York 10014
www.penguin.com
Manufactured in China
First Edition
ISBN 0-525-46854-4
2 4 6 8 10 9 7 5 3 1

CONTENTS

1, 2, 3

Kate was sitting on her front step.

"One, two, three," she said.

Along came Digby.

"Four, five, six," said Kate.

"What are you doing?" said Digby.

"I am counting," said Kate.

"Seven, eight, nine…"

Digby sat down next to Kate.

"Ten, eleven, twelve," said Kate.

"*Why* are you counting?" said Digby.

"I like to count," said Kate.

"It is fun."

"It is not fun to listen to,"

said Digby.

"Thirteen, fourteen, fifteen,"

said Kate.

Digby stood up.

He began to walk away.

"Where are you going?" said Kate.

"I do not like all this counting,"

said Digby.

"I am going for a walk."

"Oh," said Kate.

"I want to come too."

"Okay," said Digby.

"But no counting."

"No counting," said Kate.

"I promise."

Kate stood up.

The two friends began to walk.

"This is nice," said Digby.

"A…B…C…D…" said Kate.

THE PIANO

One day Kate went to Digby's house.

"Digby," she said,

"can you come out to play?"

"Not now," said Digby.

"I must practice the piano."

"But you did that yesterday,"

said Kate.

"I must do it every day," said Digby.

Kate sat down to wait.

Digby began to practice.

He played low notes.

He played high notes.

He played low notes

and high notes together.

He worked very hard.

Digby was happy.

He liked to practice the piano.

Kate was not happy.

"This is no fun," she said.

"When are you going

to play *real* music?"

"I am not ready yet," said Digby.

"Well, *I* am," said Kate.

She closed Digby's practice book.

"Now," she said,

"play some real music."

Digby got up from the piano.

He went over to his radio.

He turned it on.

"Do you like this music?" said Digby.

Kate began to dance.

"Yes," she said. "I do."

"Good," said Digby.

He gave Kate the headphones.

Kate kept dancing.

She was happy.

Digby went back to his piano.

He sat down.

Digby was happy too.

 # THAT MOUSE

Kate was sitting by a little hole

in her wall.

"That mouse is driving me crazy,"

she said.

"Why?" said Digby.

"Because I cannot catch him," said Kate.

"I try and try,

but he always gets away."

Digby lay down

next to Kate.

"I have an idea," he said.

"Maybe you can be friends

with that mouse."

"What?" said Kate.

"I like that mouse," said Digby.

"I think he would be

a good little friend."

"How can you say that?" said Kate.

"Well," said Digby,

"the mouse is smart.

And he is quiet.

And he is cute."

Kate looked at the mouse hole.

Then she looked at Digby.

"Maybe you are right," she said.

"The mouse *is* cute.

Maybe he *would* be

a good little friend."

24

Kate moved closer

to the mouse hole.

The mouse came to his door.

"See?" said Digby.

"He wants to be your friend."

Kate smiled at the mouse.

The mouse took a little step

out of his house.

"Digby," said Kate,

"that mouse is so cute,

I could eat him up."

Kate tried to grab the mouse.

She was fast.

But the mouse was faster.

"Oh, no," said Digby.

"My idea was not very good."

"Oh, yes it was," said Kate.

"This time I almost got

that mouse."

BOOTS

It was a rainy day.

Then the rain stopped.

Kate looked out her window.

Everything was wet.

"Good," said Kate.

"I can go for a walk.

I can wear my new red boots.

They will keep my feet

nice and dry."

Kate pulled the new boots on.

"Perfect!"

She went outside.

"I will go to Digby's house," she said.

Kate began to walk.

Soon she came to a big puddle.

"It's a good thing

I wore my new boots," said Kate.

"My feet will stay

nice and dry."

She waded through

the puddle.

Some water splashed her pants.

Kate walked on.

Soon she came to a bigger puddle.

"It's a good thing

I wore my new boots," said Kate.

"My feet will stay

nice and dry."

She skipped through

the puddle.

Some water splashed her jacket.

Kate walked on.

Soon she came to the biggest puddle of all.

"It's a good thing

I wore my new boots," said Kate.

"My feet will stay

nice and dry."

She jumped into the middle

of the puddle.

SPLASH!

"That was fun," said Kate.

Then she ran to Digby's house.

35

Digby came to his door.

"Oh, my!" he said.

"Look, Digby," said Kate.

"It's a good thing

I wore my new boots."

She pulled the boots off.

"My feet are nice and dry."

🐈 COPYCAT 🐈

38

Digby and Kate were sitting

in Digby's garden.

They were reading books.

Kate closed her book.

"I am done," she said.

"Now we can go for a walk."

"*You* can go for a walk,"

said Digby.

"I will stay here.

I want to finish my book."

Kate pulled Digby's arm.

"Come with me," she said.

But Digby would not

go with Kate.

"Stop pulling me," he said.

"Stop pulling me," said Kate.

"I am *not* pulling you," said Digby.

"I am *not* pulling you," said Kate.

"Copycat," said Digby.

"Copy*dog*," said Kate.

"That is not funny," said Digby.

"That is not funny," said Kate.

"Stop copying me," said Digby.

"Stop copying me," said Kate.

Digby closed his book.

He was angry.

He went into his house.

"I will read in here," he said.

He closed his door.

BANG!

Now Kate was alone.

"Digby," she called.

"I am sorry.

Open the door."

ring
bell
↓

Digby did not open his door.

"Go away," he said.

"I am reading."

Kate sat down.

"Digby is not my friend," she said.

"He told me to go away."

Kate was sad.

Digby opened his door.

"Kate," he said,

"I cannot read

when you are sad."

"Digby," said Kate,

"I cannot go for a walk

 when you are angry."

"What can we do?" said Digby.

"I have an idea," said Kate.

"We can eat lunch."

"That is a great idea," said Digby.

"And after lunch," said Kate,

"we can go for a walk."

"Okay," said Digby.

"As soon as I finish my book."